FIRST CHRISTMAS

a novella

Katharine E. Smith

Heddon Publishing

First edition published in 2023 by Heddon Publishing.

ISBN Hardcover 978-1-913166-82-3
ISBN Paperback 978-1-913166-83-0
ISBN Ebook 978-1-913166-84-7

Cover by Catherine Clarke Design
www.catherineclarkedesign.co.uk

www.heddonpublishing.com
www.facebook.com/heddonpublishing
@PublishHeddon

Katharine E. Smith is the author of sixteen novels, including the bestselling Coming Back to Cornwall series.

First Christmas is a festive novella set at the beautiful Soulton Long Barrow. It is also an introduction to a brand-new series.

A Philosophy graduate, Katharine initially worked in the IT and charity sectors. She turned to freelance editing in 2009, which led to her setting up Heddon Publishing, working with independent authors across the globe.

Katharine lives in Shropshire, UK, with her husband, their two children, and two excitable dogs.

You can find details of her books on her website:

www.katharineesmith.com

Information about her work with other authors can be found here:

www.heddonpublishing.com

and

www.heddonbooks.com

For Mum,
always

Soulton Long Barrow

This very special place which has inspired the setting for First Christmas lies just outside the small market town of Wem in North Shropshire, on land opposite Soulton Hall. The long barrow is a modern memorial based on an ancient concept. It provides a unique, secular space, with two beautifully built stone chambers which are lined with individual niches where cremations urns can be placed.

I first visited the long barrow during summer 2020, when the world was locked down and when my mum was very ill. She died a few days later.

I was struck immediately by the peace of the place and the feeling of walking into the barrow, going from the sounds of the outside world into the comforting quiet of the chambers. Since my first visit, I've been back numerous times, for the summer and winter solstices (the two ends of the barrow are aligned for these, so that the barrow floods with light if the weather is kind), for live theatre performances (as an aside, Soulton Hall and the family who live there have been linked with Shakespeare, particularly *As You Like It*), and for lots of walks with my dogs. I was also lucky enough to be able to place a stone in the roof of the second, larger chamber, and my initials are hidden within that amazing structure.

It is incredibly beautiful all year round and the farmland that the barrow is set within is looked after with careful consideration of the natural world, so close encounters with wildlife are not unusual.

 I have wanted to write about the long barrow for some time, but I am always aware that it has very personal relevance for the families who have niches there, so I wanted to make sure it was right and hopefully reflects how positive and unique this place and community are.

You can find out more about Soulton Long Barrow on the Soulton Hall and Sacred Stones websites:

www.soultonhall.co.uk

www.sacredstones.co.uk

First
Christmas

Christmas morning

A shooting star.

The very best way to start Christmas Day.

Firing across the velvet darkness before the light seeps in and the world awakes. Having said that, if my family are anything to go by, there will be multitudes of households already awake by now, over-excited children checking the ends of their beds or the floor outside their bedroom doors, to see if 'he's been'. Then comes the battle…

"Go back to bed. It's still dark." Bleary-eyed parents.

"But we can't sleep… can we just open one present? Just one?" Determined children. There is no chance they're going back to sleep. They know it. Their parents know it.

"Go on then, just one." A half-hearted attempt to buy just a few more minutes' shut-eye.

A gasp. "Look what Santa brought me! Look, Mummy."

A soft groan is emitted. The sound of defeat. A bedside light is switched on. A watch checked, disbelievingly. A double-take. *Urgh.* But then... a smile slowly crawls across her face. Remembering what it is to be a child on Christmas morning. "Let's see. Oh, that's lovely!"

A nudge of the dad, head still fuzzy from Santa's whisky, optimistically thinking he can get away with a few moments more; Mummy seems to have things covered. No chance.

Those days are long-gone for me, though. And out here, Christmas morning means peace. The road across the fields, which often carries trucks and lorries, tractors and morning commuters, is silent. Except for one car, and I know who that will be. It means she is coming. I knew that she would. We hear the trudging of her boots along the stony path outside, long before she reaches us.

"Here she comes," I say, with a little thrill of excitement.

"Here she comes," they agree. They've seen it all before, but it is new to me.

I hear her voice, as she pushes the number keys on the lock. I can see she's brought her parents along. Or, more likely, they've insisted on accompanying her. I don't blame them; I wouldn't have wanted Annie or Kitty, or Tom for that matter, coming up here alone in the dark.

Teresa, one of my fellow residents, is at Cecily's

shoulder and she breathes softly against her ear, so that the young woman turns, and she sees it: the star.

"How did you do that?" I whisper to Teresa. "How did you know it was coming?"

She shrugs, but I can tell she enjoys my admiration. "Just a feeling. It comes with time." She's a gem, is Teresa, and she's made things so much easier for me than they might have been, but she does like to make sure we know she's an old hand at all this.

"Did you see that?" Cecily asks her parents, who smile tolerantly at their only daughter's excitement.

"No... what?" asks her dad.

"A star! A shooting star!"

Her mum and dad look at each other and shake their heads. They don't understand why she loves this place so much. They're not really sure it's healthy for her, such a young woman surrounded by so much death. But, as she tells them (regularly), this is actually a place teeming with life. Enclosed snugly on farmland, where the cycle of life is never-ending, and nature and wildlife are loved and actively welcomed, the long barrow has been designed to slide in amongst all this with the minimum of fuss. Long grasses and wildflowers grow across the top of it. Approaching for the first time, it is incredible to find what lies below the two mounds; skilfully crafted stone chambers with spiralling ceilings, and doorways each end which align with the sun for the winter and summer solstices. I believe that as soon as you enter the long barrow, you find peace. I certainly did, at a point in my life which often felt anything but peaceful.

Brought in a wheelchair, by that point the effort of even the short walk from the parking spot too much, I felt something shift within me as I crossed the threshold. Graham, pushing the chair, was behind me, and the kids behind him, so I could not see their reactions, but I heard an exclamation from Kitty, and I was glad. It reinforced my own reaction. On a dry summer day, leaving the heat of the sun, the cool air felt like a soft, gentle kiss on my skin, and all outside sounds were banished.

I emerged into the first, small, round chamber, which I had seen on the website, where occupied niches were closed off with individual doors, each personal to the people they belong to. I had seen them in photos but had not really contemplated what they signified. That each enclosed, each signified, a life, or lives. Behind the beautifully designed and crafted fronts were urns, bearing ashes, of people who had lived, and died. And I knew that soon that would be me – either in the barrow, or some place else. Somewhere that my family were so keen that I should choose, although on my darker days I wondered what the point would be.

Still, the quiet, contemplative peace of the barrow welcomed us, and I felt all of my resolve and my determination to be strong melt away. My tears fell freely. I knew that it was quite alright to feel that way, that I didn't always have to be 'brave'. But still, I did not want my family to see. I wanted, very much, to be alone, for just a few minutes, and let this place help me let it all sink in. All the drama and trauma of the past few months. The shock of the diagnosis, the punch of the prognosis. The gradual ravaging, the savaging, of my body. The knowledge that I would be leaving my life and my family. All that I knew. All that I had hoped for and believed in, and poured my heart and soul into.

And then, like an angel, there she was. "Hello?" I heard her before I saw her, at the other end of the barrow, where the large stained-glass door glowed against the light. It opened, and in she came. A dark shape at first, approaching, but she carried with her a torch, and as she came closer I could make out her features. I could see she was smiling.

"You must be Ruth," she said. "I'm Cecily. One of the barrow guardians."

If she could see I was crying, she did not react to that. She just put out her hand to shake mine, and placed her other hand lightly on my shoulder.

"Would you like to come through to the second chamber?" she asked, of me and my family. "There's more space through there."

Expertly, she lit candle after candle as she led the way back through the short corridor, which was also lined with niches – many empty, but some occupied, and as we followed on and I emerged into the second, larger chamber, which Cecily was nimbly navigating and filling with the warm candlelight, I gasped. Above was a high roof constructed entirely from the same rich, creamy stone that the rest of the barrow is built from, painstakingly laid in a concentric design. It was almost dizzying to look at.

My family walked carefully, reverentially, in, their feet crunching on the gravel floor. They looked around them – each, I knew, considering different elements. Graham – the niches. Estimating their size. Their material. His eyes expertly assessing their angles and dimensions. Annie – the roof. The incredible engineering feat. So different to her own work, but very much to be admired. Kitty – the artwork. The painting of the blackbird. The stained glass. The metalwork. Tom, meanwhile, was seeking something less tangible. He was breathing slowly. Listening. Trying to capture, to understand, the feeling of the space we were occupying.

Cecily stood back, her hands folded neatly before her and her gaze for the most part on the floor, although I noticed she took the chance to look at each of my family in turn, and when she saw me looking, she smiled. "If you have any questions, just ask. I know you will have, but take your time. Look around the barrow, and go and explore outside too if you like. Lots of our families like to come and spend time here. They… well, I'll tell you more later. In fact, I'll go and sit outside, and you can come and find me when you're ready."

"Mum?" Kitty asked, coming to the front of me. "What do… what do you think?"

"I think…" I said slowly, reluctant to commit to anything definite. Not wanting to be rushed, even though I recognised what a relief it would be to them, to have just this one thing sorted and settled. "I think it is beautiful. I think it is peaceful, and I think it is in a wonderful place." I realised I meant all of this, very much, and that actually, I could see myself making a decision, there and then. This momentous choice which I now realise is far more important for them than for me. I dried my tears carefully, and surreptitiously, so that I was ready for my family, when they needed me.

"Do you have any questions we could ask that girl?" Annie asked.

"She's not a girl!" Kitty needled. "She's a young woman, like you and me. Well... I'm young anyway."

"Kitty..." I said warningly, but I was glad to see Annie actually smile.

"You're right, Kit, sorry. I think... she just seems so young, for all of this." Annie gestured around us, and I knew what she meant.

"But she seems very good," I said. "And I suppose it's a calling, to be able to do this. You would have to be somebody special."

"I don't know that I could do it," Kitty said.

"I definitely couldn't," Annie admitted. "Not for me, at all. But it is a good place, Mum."

"But it's so remote," Graham spoke at last. "You'd be... it's just... so far away."

"It's not, love. Not really." I reached for his hand, which felt cool, and too thin. He'd been losing weight, not as much as I had, but the stress was killing his appetite, and eating up his energy. "It feels like it, because it's out here in the middle of the farmland, but that road's just ten minutes' walk away, and home's only another five minutes by car. And besides, you like remote. You always have. So do I."

"Yes, but I like remote with you," he said forlornly. It felt like somebody had squeezed my heart with their fist. I folded his fingers in mine, and I tried to find his gaze. Being in a wheelchair is frustrating for so many reasons. Not being able to stand and hug somebody when they need it – to let them lean on you – is just one of them.

"Tom?" I said, gulping back the lump in my throat. "What do you think?"

"I think… it's what you said, Mum. It's peaceful. It's… special."

"It is. I really think it is. So," ever the practical one, I drew up all the energy I could muster, and asked them, "what do we want to know? Forget the financial side of things. We know how much this costs. What about how and when you can visit? Who has access? What about having a ceremony here? How secure is this place?"

"I was thinking along those lines, Mum," Annie said approvingly.

"Come on then, let's go and find Cecily," Kitty said. "And let's get back out into the sunshine for a while, shall we?"

"Yes," I said, although a part of me wanted to stay a while longer amid the tranquillity. But there would, I reasoned, be time enough for that.

Now, I know this place inside-out. And as Cecily enters the barrow, with her usual respectful manner, she first lights the candles in front of the occupied niches, quietly wishing each of us a happy Christmas. Her parents, standing in the entranceway, smile indulgently at their kind, gentle daughter. We, in turn, smile indulgently at them. They don't know the truth of this place. We see that, and Cecily knows it too, but she never stops trying to show them.

Who is the 'we' to whom I refer? You may well be wondering. Well, there are another twenty or so souls here at this long barrow – although you must understand we are not confined to this place, or this space. We do not sit each in our allocated niches, awaiting visitors. It is not a hospital ward. It is all symbolism; the niches, and the urns in which our ashes reside. We are not just here at the barrow; we are everywhere, where we choose to be. It's impossible to explain to somebody who has not experienced it. I always knew, even as a schoolgirl attending Sunday School, that humans did not, could not, hold the key to everything. They could not possibly know everything about the universe. Why should they?

Still, the barrow is a home – or a home from home, as Teresa calls it. She was the first one here; the first of us to occupy a niche.

"Was it lonely?" I asked her.

"Well no," she says, "not exactly. Although it was strange. Learning to navigate this new… situation. You know what it's like."

I do. But I won't dwell on that now.

Funnily enough, I already knew Teresa. Not well, but our paths had crossed, a number of times. But I didn't know she had died, so that should give you some idea of how well I knew her. It's like that round here. The town we live(d) in is small enough that you recognise so many people, without even thinking about it – and there are many people that you pass in the street regularly but it might never even occur to you that you had not seen them in a while. Still, it was good to see a familiar face.

As well as Teresa, the people I spend the most time with here are a similar age to me; or were a similar age when they died: David, Kiran, and a couple called – I kid you not – Terry and June. When I met them, I laughed at their names. "Yes, like the TV show!" June had said, smiling. "Thank god you're old enough to remember!"

Jasmine, a young woman who had not quite made it to thirty, smiled. "They were so disappointed when they could see it meant nothing to me!"

"It's true," Terry said fondly. "They don't know what they've missed out on. Don't make programmes like that anymore."

"No, and for good reason," said Adam, another of the younger ones, although apparently he could remember his parents watching it. "What was that other one? With Michael Spencer?"

"Frank Spencer!" Terry had corrected him. "Played by Michael Crawford. That's where you're getting confused. Anyway, it was *Some Mothers Do 'Ave 'Em*. Ooh, Betty."

Adam and Jasmine had looked at each other and laughed, but not unkindly.

Teresa had put a guiding arm around me (that's the best way I can think of to explain it, but it's not quite like you're imagining). "I think we're going a bit off-topic here," she said. "And Ruth needs some time to settle in. Find out what it's all about. She's probably not too worried about TV at the moment."

We all rub along; we are building a community. Some of us, like me, actively chose to be a part of this. Some of us have had their ashes brought here upon much reflection on the part of family, partners and friends. David, for instance, died a long time before any of the rest of us, but his wife could not bear to be parted from his ashes and had no idea what to do with them anyway.

"I didn't want to scatter them," she has said to David on one of her visits – the rest of us made ourselves scarce so that he could sit with her in peace, but not before she had begun this line of monologue. "I didn't want to lose you completely."

I understand. It's part of what makes this place so special. Our ashes are kept here, in their entirety, or even just in part. Some have been made into jewellery, or divided between offspring, to do with as they please. I have no problem with this. Whatever makes the pain more bearable. Those ashes are not us anyway; they are a mere representation. We live on, we reside, entirely separately from them. Our families may visit, and take our urns outside – their wish is to include us in a picnic, say, or take us for a walk through the countryside. It brings some solace to them, but it's not us that they carry with them. We can choose to accompany them or not, and of course the majority of us choose to, most of the time.

Today, they will all come, or most of them, so Teresa tells me. It's my first Christmas here, so I'm about to find out. So many occasions bring them here. Birthdays, anniversaries and other significant dates. Christmas is apparently the big one, when the barrow is as busy as it ever gets – even counting the solstices.

As Cecily stands back and admires the effect of so many candles, flames shimmering and dancing, choreographed by the very slight breeze that we create just for her, the church bells chime across the field; heralding the coming of Our Saviour, if you believe in that stuff – and ringing in the one day of the year when the majority of the population feel justified in staying in. Fires going, kitchens over-worked – (mostly) mothers, too. A cosy, happy, magical day. Unless…

I always knew there could be occasions when Christmas was anything but happy. And there comes a time for many of us – a threshold we cross – after which it will never be the same again. I knew that, when my parents died, and my sister. I kept it going for the kids; kept the smile in place, and traditions alive, but I was relieved when it was over. I could never again feel the magic in the same way.

Now it pains me to think that my own children know that feeling. I hope that somehow my family find it within themselves to enjoy this day, no matter what. And although I know where they are, what they are doing, right now – I can sit with them as they eat their breakfast, each trying not to think too hard about previous Christmas mornings – the part of the day I am most looking forward to is when they come out here.

First will be Kitty. She is not the first of all the visitors to arrive – that award goes to Teresa's partner, Val, and Teresa's son, Derek. He does not look like a Derek. Teresa has confessed that she hates his name but was pressured into it by her evil (as she calls her) ex-mother-in-law and pathetic mummy's boy of an ex-husband. "Baby Derek!" she laughs now. "It just sounded wrong. But it's his name, and it's grown on me. After all, it's part and parcel of who he is."

They pass Cecily on their way in; at the sound of incomers, she and her parents have stepped sensitively outside, knowing that there are others now to mind the space – and knowing that

Cecily's forethought in arriving beforehand, and lighting up the place, will create a welcoming atmosphere on this often difficult day. Val and Derek greet them as they cross paths, and then come in cheerily, as though popping across to visit one's late partner's or late mother's ashes is the most natural thing in the world. And Val cradles Teresa's urn while Derek pours coffee from a flask. It smells good. Expensive. Teresa confirms it will be. She sits between them and I am sure they know she's there.

"That's good," breathes Val, as she takes a sip, and I can almost taste the strong, bitter flavour. I miss that physical sensation, and the feeling of heat flowing through me when the coffee is just the exact right temperature.

"Mmm," Derek agrees, and then they are both quiet for a while. Sipping their drinks contemplatively, the cheer gone for the moment. They are reflecting on Christmases past.

Val remembers her first Christmas with Teresa, when they'd all but split up and then Teresa had shown up at her front door, bearing flowers and champagne, and a Christmas pudding far too large for her and Derek. He was in the car, waiting to see what would happen with his mum and her friend. When they kissed, he was not surprised, but he knew that he didn't want the boys at school to find out.

He now is remembering his childhood Christmases. Not just Christmas Day itself – in fact, that might have been his least favourite of all, having to mind his manners for his dad and his grandma, sitting straight at the table and making polite conversation (or at least politely answering the questions that were barked at him), but he loved the breaks from school. Those blessed times when he felt absolutely sure of the world and his place in it.

He had not enjoyed school. It was the one his dad had gone to, and his dad's dad before him. Derek had to board there during the week, although his mum hated it as much as he did. The sacred Christmas holidays meant freedom, and time with his mum, and sometimes his cousins and aunts and uncles, while his dad mainly worked – away, if Derek was really lucky. He remembers cosy, intimate times cooking with his mum, in a kitchen with steamed-up windows. Staying up late reading, knowing that he had no dorm mates to worry about, and no lessons to get up for in the morning. Those late nights were deliciously liberating, and refreshing.

I feel guilty knowing all this, and I leave them

to it. "Enjoy," I say to Teresa, and I begin to feel a little thrill of excitement at the thought of my own visitors. Even though I can see them any time I like, it's knowing that they are coming here, to see me. It reminds me of when the kids had first left home – to uni in Annie and Tom's case, and work for Kitty – and they'd come back for weekends. Only this time I don't have the chance to irritate them with lots of questions. This time, they will miss those questions, and they will wish that I could irritate them again.

Kitty

She has driven across here from her flat and she's planning to stay overnight in the family home, where Graham is currently having breakfast with Annie and Alex. Tom will be here next. He's walking, with Mavis. My beloved spaniel. But first it is Kitty, and I'm glad of the chance to see her alone, as I know she is glad to have some time here alone, too. She glances shyly at Derek and Val, and greets them in her sweet, quiet fashion, then she approaches my niche, self-consciously.

Lovely Val suggests to Derek that they take Teresa outside 'for some fresh air' and then Kitty relaxes, just a little. And now I am aware of the others here; that just as I knew what Derek and Val were thinking about, they could be cognisant of Kitty's thoughts and feelings. And what a heart-wrenching tangle they are. Not only has she lost me, her mum, this year, but her long-term relationship has broken down too. Not a bad thing, in my opinion. Olly was a pain in the arse. Very moody. But still, it's a blow for her, and she has had to dig deep to find a way through these last few months. I'm so glad she's got her friends around her, and of course her family. No matter how much Annie and Kitty get on each other's nerves, they always look out for each other. As for Tom, well he's everyone's baby. A key ally for the girls whenever they fell out, growing up – or a toy, a plaything; to be dressed up, stuffed in the old pushchair. Babied.

As Kitty sits heavily on the stone ledge in front of my niche, I try to wreath around her, like a supernatural hug. Hugs are another thing I miss from the physical world. I recall those days when the children were little and off school ill, and all they would want was to sit cuddling into me, watching TV, or dozing off while I read. Those days were a break from the daily grind of school/work/home and although I would of course not have wished my children illness, they were special times. I could press my lips to their hot, clammy foreheads, or the top of their hair, smelling their very particular, individual, familiar scent. I would breathe in, softly; try to etch the moment into my mind. I'm glad to say that it worked. Those memories are as real to me now as anything, though those days are long since passed.

Now, Kitty stills. Has she felt it? My presence? But her shoulders slump, and her head falls into her hands, and she lets it all out. Great, heavy wracking sobs and tears. It's good for her. It's necessary. But still, it is hard to see.

And then, just like that, she stops it. Like pushing a cork back into a bottle. She is, I know, aware of Val and Derek nearby, and she does not want anyone to witness her grief. If only she knew how many of us there are here. We all see it. We all sympathise, and some of the others offer sympathy to me.

"We've all been there," June tells me kindly. "It happens, and not even just early on. It might be something else in their lives, in later years, that triggers it, and they find their way back here, back to you, and let it all out. They're free to let go here. It's a safe space, away from reality."

Kitty, I try my hardest to reach her, but I don't think that it works. *Kitty, my love.*

She was a sweet, sweet child, and she has grown into an equally sweet young woman. All of my children loved animals, but Kitty more than the others put together. Now she's trying to carve out a career as an artist, and she works at a dog kennels and rescue centre, and paints pet portraits to earn some extra cash. Somehow, she manages it, paying her rent alone now that Olly has gone. Graham has helped her as well, and rightly so. Tom moved home, before I became ill, so he's living rent-free, while money is not something Annie is in need of. She has other requirements.

We always said we would support our children in any way we could, whenever we could. Financially, emotionally... physically, if we had to. This is not to say we don't want them to be independent, but we brought them into this world and if we could help them in any way when times were tough, we would.

Through school, Kitty had a large group of friends – always girls and boys, even at the more difficult ages – and was never short of invitations to parties or sleepovers. But her eyes were open to the nuances of changing friendships and power plays. Annie was less widely popular with her friends and there was one New Year's Eve when she was twenty, back from her first term at uni, and Kitty had just turned eighteen. Kitty had a party lined up to go to but then Annie was let down by her friends, and Kitty changed her own plans to go out with her sister. Graham and I had waited up for them, and it was a joy to see them arrive home at 2am, rosy-faced and laughing. We discovered later that the girls had been around the various local pubs (there are quite a number for such a small town) and stopped and chatted to friends and neighbours, who were charmed, and commended Graham and me on the children we had brought up. Of course, that's not our credit to claim, but it was a lovely thing to hear.

The next day, the girls fell out over something trivial – I can't remember what – but that's siblings for you. I just know that, whatever, they will never fall out so badly that it can't be fixed.

I can sense indecision in Kitty now; a hesitation, not sure what to do here all on her own. And she hears the voices, too, of Terry and June's family arriving; their son Mark, his wife Sally, and their children. The boy clutches a shiny toy car, and remote control, while his mum tells him this is 'not the place' for it. In fact, it could be, if it wouldn't bother anyone else. This should be a place that people feel happy, or at the very least comfortable, coming to.

They fall quiet as they see Kitty sitting alone, but she puts on her best smile. "Happy Christmas!" she says.

"Happy Christmas," they reply, all except their little girl, Samantha, who looks shyly at Kitty and squeezes her mum's hand.

"Come on," Mark says, "let's find Granny and Grandad, shall we? Can you remember where they are?"

Terry and June look on with perfect proud-grandparent expressions. Kitty stands, and wanders outside, yawning and stretching as she walks into the light. Not knowing what else to do, she finds the large bag she has left outside and checks its contents, then she sits on one of the rough-hewn benches and watches the birds flitting about in the large oak tree that partially covers the pond outside the barrow. The branches are bare now, but only just, and the dry, crinkly brown leaves litter the ground and float like delicate toy boats across the surface of the water. The winter has not yet turned cold and even today, the sun warms Kitty's face as she sits and patiently lets time tiptoe by. The light breeze touches her skin, and I try to be a part of it, to make her feel my presence with her. Maybe she does. She closes her eyes for a moment and thinks of me. Not the ill me, but the me from before. In our warm, cosy kitchen, putting the kettle on. Is that how they remember me? I like to believe that there was much more to me than that but it's emblematic, I suppose, of my role for them. Making them at home. Providing comfort and a moment of being looked after. A safe place to come to when the world outside is scary.

And now, she's remembering a trip to London, to the theatre, and around the shops. That was a happy day. Just me and her.

Now, she's thinking of how it felt to lean against me, and recalling the time that George, her first guinea pig, died, and how she had sobbed into my chest, her tears sinking into the soft wool of my jumper.

It is both a privilege and a responsibility to be able to know what my children are thinking, as I longed to be able to do during my life with them. I am careful not to over-use it. I close myself off from my daughter's internal world and just sit beside her. Waiting for my son, her brother, and an over-excited spaniel to arrive on the scene.

Tom

Oh, Tom. My beautiful boy. The girls, when they were feeling grumpy, or looking for something to feel put-out about, would say I favoured him above them. It isn't true, or at least I hope it isn't. I really do love all three children equally. I recognise their faults, and they quite freely recognised mine, but that doesn't detract from the love.

Tom, though, was easy, in a way that the girls just weren't. Even Kitty, who I have described as sweet, had her moments, and plenty of them. It's part and parcel of being a teenage girl. I always knew that. But there were days when I just didn't have it in me, to be everything they expected me to be. And at times it felt like Tom was the only person who asked me how I was. Graham was often tied up with work and the girls involved in the complex business of being teenagers. Tom, who was no angel by the way, would sometimes just seem to know if I needed a hug, or would ask if I'd had a good day. Yes, possibly it was when he wanted something, but that may be doing him a disservice.

He is a one-off, and was popular at school but not one for having a best friend. In fact, he often spent more time with girls, throughout primary and secondary; he was not into sport, and he was not much into computer games either. He's always had a love of music, and the natural world, which seem to go quite well together. And I think those two things are what make him feel so comfortable here at the barrow as well. He comes often, usually with Mavis, the pair of them rambling along the public rights of way and then along past the standing stones which mark the path.

"Hello Mum," he'll say, once he's wrangled with the lock (you can add practical skills to the list of areas in which he is somewhat lacking). He'll have tied Mavis to the bench outside, and he'll come lolloping into the long barrow, his fringe in his eyes and his lopsided smile on his face. He will look around, and say "Hi all of you too," or words to that effect – which has endeared him greatly to my fellow residents – and then he'll open the niche, lift out the urn, and bring me outside. Mavis will have a good sniff of the urn, though I can't believe it bears any scent of me, and then Tom will place it on the bench next to him, pull a bottle of water, a bowl, a flask of tea and some biscuits from his bag, and the two of them will enjoy a drink, sharing the stash of snacks. He is quite content to spend time that way, and his work, as a hospital porter, means that he does odd shifts and is often available for daytime visits.

He might pull a notepad from his bag, and jot down wildlife sightings or observations. If he spots something in the distance, he'll fish out his binoculars and occasionally give a soft exclamation. He greets birds and insects warmly and gently, offering a 'hello there' to a buzzard sailing silently above, or a kestrel aloft on the currents. He has lately developed a particular liking for seagulls and I think he fancies that they may be a sign from me, with my love of the sea. He remembers me telling him that people used to believe seagulls are the souls of sailors lost at sea. He also remembers himself haughtily telling me that there are no such thing as seagulls, just gulls: "The 'sea' part is only relevant if they actually live near the sea." He cringes now when he thinks of it. I want to tell him it doesn't matter. It really doesn't.

They all do it, my family, and some of my friends, too; remembering mis-spoken words or stupid arguments, but really and truly, they are of no importance now.

"Kitty!" She and I hear his voice before we see him emerging around the side of the barrow, Mavis pulling at her lead, tongue lolling in her determination to get to my daughter.

"Tom!" my daughter says, so relieved to have a comrade. "Hello Mavis!" she says, laughing as she hugs her little brother before crouching to see the dog. Mavis puts muddy paws on Kitty's knees so she can lick her face. Kitty just laughs; if she were Annie, this would have provoked an entirely different reaction.

"Happy Christmas," Kitty says.

"Yes, and to you. I keep forgetting it's Christmas, weirdly."

"I know," Kitty says sadly. "It doesn't feel like it somehow, does it? I kind of just want to get it over and done with."

"Yeah, I know what you mean. I've been dreading it. I've tried not to, but I can't help it."

I remember saying to both of these two when I was ill how everything had happened since Christmas. We had a lovely one last year; we were all together for it, and I'm so grateful that we were. But it struck me how it was just a month or so later that I was handed my diagnosis, and how everything seemed to snowball from there. Now, I wish that I hadn't said those words. I know they both remember them, and the Christmas element has even more significance for them.

"How's Dad?" asks Kitty.

"Oh, he's trying to put a brave face on it. But he's not very good at it!" They both laugh.

"It's awful, isn't it? Do you think we should have just gone away? Done something completely different?"

"I don't know. I don't think anything would make things any better. Wherever he is, whatever he's doing, he'll be wishing Mum was with him."

I know this is true, and it's no surprise to me, but still these words are a blow. Graham is not the first person to be bereaved of their spouse; not by a long, long way, but still I wish it had not happened to him. Which I suppose means that I wish he had died first, and that is not true either, but I would wish to spare him from this immense, intense pain, if I could. I have been spared, by being the one to go first, but I wonder if I would have been quite as lost without him. Now I'll never know.

"Is Mum still in there?" Tom jerks his head towards the barrow.

"Erm… yeah." Kitty is not keen on calling the ashes 'Mum'. She does not think of them as me, and she's right not to. But Tom takes a certain pride in his confidence, his ease, with this place, and with which he can open the door to the niche and lift my urn carefully, bringing it outside – like a proud father emerging from the hospital with his newborn. It seems brave to him, and reflects his comfort with the prospect of death. Except I know that to some extent this is only surface-deep and that within him he is as scared as anyone. He is just trying his best to do the right thing, and look at things the right way. Just as I know that he's lonely, and he'd love to find a girlfriend, but he won't admit that to anyone. It's such a clichéd way to feel, and the last thing Tom ever wants to be is a cliché.

Our marriage probably seemed very staid and boring to Tom, but I do hope that he appreciates the stability it provided for him and his sisters as they grew up and into themselves. And we never tried to stop Tom being what he wanted to be, although Graham would often fret that he was wasting a perfectly good brain. Late at night, we'd have whispered conversations, where Graham would convey his fears to me, but I'd tell him the same as I had with the girls as well: "Allow them to find their own way. Let them be themselves. Just make sure they know that we're here for them, no matter what."

Kitty sits back down on the bench and holds Mavis' lead while Tom goes into the barrow, and can't help smiling into the space around him. The voices of Terry and June's family echo from within the larger chamber and Tom considers shouting through a cheery hello, but thinks better of it.

Instead, he opens up the niche, lifts the earthenware container carefully out, then returns to the outside world, places the urn next to Kitty, and sits on the other side of it. Kitty's left hand touches the top of the urn, as she hopes to find something; some connection, or comfort, but it just feels cold.

"Mulled wine?" she asks.

"You haven't!"

"I have!"

I already know about this, of course. Kitty has been up early, carefully following my recipe, and filling all the flasks she could find (some she had borrowed from Graham but didn't tell him why). She pulls one out now and pours a cup each for herself and her brother.

The steam and the scent of the spices rise into the air. Tiny insects buzz and hum above it, illuminated in the rays of the sun.

"Nice one, sis. Happy Christmas!"

"Happy Christmas, Tom. Happy Christmas, Mum." Tears glisten in her eyes as she says these last three words, and Tom reaches out to his sister, pulling her to him, and the pair of them hug for a few moments, the urn pressed between them.

As they sip their drinks, each lost in their own thoughts, Derek and Val return from their walk.

"Would you like some mulled wine?" Kitty asks them.

They look at each other.

"That would be lovely!" says Val.

Kitty pours them a cup each. "One flask down," she says.

"Oh, have we finished your wine?" Derek asks.

"Plenty more where that came from," Kitty grins, pulling down the top of the bag and revealing another six flasks. That's my girl.

"Class!" Derek says, and grins at her.

As Mark and his family emerge into the sunlight, Kitty offers them a cup too.

"Just a small one," says Sally. "Drawn the short straw!"

"We're off to the in-laws after this," Mark confides.

The children run off, glad to be out in the open, and the six adults make a surprisingly merry group. They talk about Christmases past and Tom, as always, draws the conversation round to music, which turns out to be a passion of Val's.

"We should have had a carol concert here," she says.

"We still could!" Tom says, all boyish enthusiasm. "Tonight! What about it?"

"I don't know, Tom, people will have their own plans," Kitty cautions.

"I'd be up for it," shrugs Val.

"Me too," says Derek.

Mark looks at Sally. "What about your parents?" he asks. "Would they mind?"

"I think they might quite like it, too," she says. "It can't hurt to ask."

Kitty, like me, is thinking that Annie isn't going to like this idea. Graham... who knows? At the moment, he'll go along with anything, as long as he isn't alone. But the decision, it seems, has been made, and the idea is already taking shape.

"I'll bring my guitar!" Tom says.

"Fantastic," Val gushes. "I'm sure Teresa will love it," she says, kissing the urn which she is holding tight to her chest.

I look at Teresa and raise my eyebrows. She just smiles, and places a fond kiss on Val's forehead.

Annie

By the time Annie arrives, with Alex and Graham, the barrow is alive with visitors. I've never seen so many at the same time, although of course I've not been here all that long. Usually, guests (as I like to think of them) arrive sporadically, but of course today is an unusual day. Nobody wants to be alone at Christmas – not even the dead.

Kitty and Tom have been offering mulled wine to all and sundry, and many have accepted this kind offer, with a smile. Kitty is half-cut, in fact, having decided to leave her car here and walk back home with Tom and Mavis. *Home*, I think. It's a painful concept now, and I can't help but feel a little bit left out that I can't really call it that anymore. Now, home is this long barrow. I've been moved out, moved on. It's silly, of course. But life has already progressed for my family and major events have happened without me. Kitty splitting up with Olly, for one. Tom getting his job at the hospital. Reasons for celebrations (and pretend-commiserations in Kitty's place, but secretly everyone is jubilant that she's kicked her boyfriend into touch) to which I am not party. Not really. I cannot advise them on their choices, I just have to observe. It's hard.

But it's not really Kitty and Tom who I worry about. I know they will be OK. It's Annie – my first-born, my hard-faced, to all intents and purposes needing-nobody daughter – who causes me the most concern. She's never found it very easy to live in the world. To share a space with other people. Almost painfully intelligent, she has yet to find those social skills so vital to a happy life. And Alex, poor Alex – stupid Alex, I also think, but don't tell anyone – puts up with a lot. And I still, even now, don't quite understand how they have ended up married. He is in awe of her, and will bend to her will, and I suppose for Annie that is quite nice. She likes to be in control. She likes to know where she stands. But I think he is also a bit scared of her. He's bright enough, and nice enough, but, well, there's never seemed to be a lot to him, if you know what I mean. The two of them met at school, they became friends, and he asked her out numerous times over the years before she said yes. Within a year, they were engaged. Within another six months, they were married. All by the age of twenty-five.

"Too young," said Graham. *Too young*, thought I (I didn't want him to know I agreed).

But married they were, and married they are. And to give them their due, it's been eight years now. Still, I cannot believe it will be for life.

Annie has hurried on ahead of her dad and her husband. She is momentarily disappointed to see her brother and sister already here, with 'me' (my urn) sitting alongside them. Also, she notes, there are other people mingling around, and they're drinking – if she is not mistaken – mulled wine. *Kitty*, she thinks, although she's half-admiring. She wishes she'd thought of it, and that she could believe she would have acted on the idea if she had.

Mavis jumps up at her, tail wagging double-speed, as though it's been days since they've seen each other, not just an hour or two.

"Annie!" Her siblings stand to hug her, and she notes that both are slightly tipsy. But she allows herself to be hugged, and she puts her arms around them both. She is the matriarch now, or the closest thing to it, if they'd only let her be so.

Not many people get away with calling her Annie. Most people are too scared, but not her brother and sister. They won't let her get away with her tough act. They know her far too well.

As Graham and Alex catch up, Kitty foists mulled wine on the three of them and then she and Tom graciously give up their seats beside the urn, insisting Graham sits and takes some moments, and Annie too. They take Alex with them as they wander along the length of the causeway that leads to the amphitheatre – an unplanned effect of the unexpected covid lockdowns, where theatre productions have been held both during and after the hell that was 'social distancing', and which is lined either side with a deep, water-filled ditch.

"How have they been?" Kitty asks Alex. "How's Dad? How's Annie?"

"Oh, you know," he says, looking at her. He takes in her concerned brown eyes, below serious brows. Alex can never get over how similar his wife and her sister look, and yet how different they are in every other way.

"No," Tom says, "we don't. That's why we're asking."

"Tom!" Kitty says, squeezing Alex's arm in hers. "Don't be mean."

Alex smiles gratefully at his sister-in-law.

"Well you were with us this morning, Tom, so yes, you do know," Alex says, pulling the older brother-in-law card out of the pack. Kitty smiles approvingly. But Alex also knows it's hard, for all of them. The first Christmas without their mum. "But they're doing OK. Not happy, but then they wouldn't be. But trying their best. Ruth would be proud."

He's right of course, but I don't really need Alex telling people how I would or wouldn't have felt. Anyway, it's not that I *would be* proud. I **am** proud.

I can see it needles Tom, too, but Kitty is more generous. She puts her arm through Alex's, and her other through Tom's. They walk together slowly back towards the barrow, where they can see Graham and Annie sitting on the bench, and it looks like more people have turned up too. They can't hear the conversation that Annie and her dad are having but I am privy to this as well.

"I don't know how I'm going to go on, Annie."

"But you don't have any choice, Dad." She steels herself; puts up the ready barriers she has long since cultivated, to protect herself from feeling too strongly. It means she can find the appropriate response, without dragging her own feelings in too close. It is only Annie that Graham would talk to like this; he loves all his children but he feels like his eldest is the one who understands him, and he appreciates her logic and steadfastness. He knows she will have sound advice, and he knows she won't tell anyone – not even Alex. Graham confided in me more than once that he has no idea how and why Annie is with Alex but, while I know what he means, he doesn't see the good points of Annie's husband, or how much that man puts up with from my headstrong, lovely, bossy, beautiful daughter.

She is loyal though, is Annie, and if anyone were to criticise Alex to her she'd jump down their throat. It's happened more than once with Tom, who sometimes just can't help himself.

"But *you're* always having a go at him," Tom pointed out once.

"No I'm not. And anyway, even if I am, he's my husband."

"Well yes, that's quite a large reason that you shouldn't always be having a go at him," Tom had countered.

"It's fine. He knows what I'm like."

"Well yes love," I had put in gently, "but maybe he could do with a bit of a break sometimes. Especially when you're around other people."

"Oh thanks, Mum," Annie had turned on me, and I saw Tom's cheeky face, grinning at me from behind her. "I'm sorry you think I'm such an awful wife."

"Annie," I'd sighed, ignoring Tom, "I didn't say that. But perhaps if you have a problem with Alex, you could talk about it when you're in private. It is a little bit awkward sometimes, you know, if you two are having an argument in front of us."

As Tom skipped off to his room, I half-cursed him for having started this. But it was something that had been on my mind, and I'd considered saying something before, many times.

"I don't think we're that bad," she said.

"You're not *bad* at all," I had replied carefully, "and we love having you here – both of you. But if you can imagine what it's like being Alex, in somebody else's home, even though he's known us for years, and you're pointing out something he's done wrong in front of us... well, it's maybe not the nicest feeling in the world."

I was being generous. She doesn't just point out things he's done wrong, she snaps at him over the smallest thing. But, like I say, if anyone else were to criticise him, she'd come down on them like a ton of bricks.

"But he can be really annoying."

Well yes, I thought, but I knew better than to say that out loud. "That's marriage, though! That's sharing your life with somebody. And I don't suppose you'd want him pointing out your faults in front of his parents, or his brother...?"

"I don't have any faults, though." She'd grinned suddenly, and shaken off all her defensiveness. This is the side of Annie that she doesn't show enough, and certainly doesn't show to enough people.

It made me smile, and I hugged her.

"I don't know why I do it, Mum," she sighed into my shoulder. "I know it's horrible. I'm a bitch."

"Well..."

She had pulled back and looked at me, and seen I was smiling.

"I know it's horrible. I'm like a pushy parent berating their child. I just... he really frustrates me sometimes."

"I would say, if you don't mind, that most people frustrate you."

"Yes, true, but I'm not married to most people. But it's not fair on Alex, I know that really. I sometimes think I expect too much."

"Only sometimes?" I wondered if I was pushing it.

"Alright, alright, I get it, Mum! Thank you." Yes, confirmation I'd taken it a bit too far.

"Annie," I'd said, seeing she was shutting down, and about to turn away. "Listen, it's hard being married. And I know it's hard being you sometimes."

Immediately on hearing these words, her eyes began to fill with tears. A very rare event, at least in front of anyone else. I'd put money on her shedding a few tears in private.

"Alex clearly loves you, and for good reason. We all love you, for that matter. You are unique, and intelligent, and fierce and strong. But you need to understand that not everyone is the same, and also that you don't have to be always fierce and strong, and especially not around us. And perhaps a little less so towards Alex."

She didn't say anything, but she didn't walk away. And I could tell she'd heard me, and she wasn't angry. It was the best I could hope for at the time. I can't say it made a lot of difference to how she behaved towards Alex but every now and then, if I thought she was being a bit much, I would catch her eye, and she'd catch my drift, and to her credit she would tone it down.

Now, as Tom, Alex and Kitty arrive back at the barrow, Alex comes behind the bench and puts his hands on Annie's shoulders. It is all she can do to prevent herself from shrugging him off. I can feel the tension in her but if he can, he doesn't show it.

"We should have a photo," Kitty, always thinking visually, suggests. "It's such a beautiful

sky, behind the barrow, and we're all here –"
'even Mum,' she wants to say, but she can't quite
bring herself to… *You don't know the half of it*, I
think – "and, I don't know, I guess it's an
important occasion. It's one to be remembered."

Nobody has the heart to say no, although I am
not sure that anyone else really wants this to
happen. Kitty looks around and sees Derek and
Val on one of the other benches. She goes across
and Val is more than happy to oblige, once Kitty's
shown her how to work her phone.

"Here you go," Val says to the family group. My
urn takes centre stage on the bench, with Kitty
and Annie squashed onto one side of it, Graham
on the other, and Tom and Alex standing behind.
Tom puts his hands on his dad's shoulders; Alex
one hand on Annie's shoulder and one on Kitty's.

I stand between Tom and Alex, and I'm aware
suddenly of Teresa at my side, and Terry and June,
and David. Adam and Jasmine appear, too.

"What are you doing?" I ask them. "This is a
family photo!" Of course I don't mind really, but
I'm a bit bemused.

"Wait and see," says Teresa, "you'll love it.
They will, too. They always do."

Adam puts his fingers in a V behind Alex's head
but Teresa shoots him a look and he stops. My

friends in death surround my family, gently, placing themselves behind them, or at their feet. They smile when Val says to and say 'cheese' when instructed. It all feels a bit odd, these familiar phrases for a wholly unfamiliar situation, and I can see Val half-regrets it, but she is committed now.

Click, click, click. There is absolutely no need for a phone to make a clicking noise when it takes a photo, but there's something quite nice about it. Old school, as Tom would say.

"Here you go," says Val, handing the phone back to Kitty. "I took a few, so hopefully there's at least one good one."

"Thank you," Kitty says, scrolling back through the images as she sits back down next to Annie. "Look at that!" she breathes. "That's weird."

I peer over her shoulder, as does Alex. The photos are beautiful, but there is an unmistakeable mist around my family, and a glow somehow – almost a rainbow effect. I turn to Teresa. "That was you?"

"That was us, my dear! All of us together. Our energies."

She follows Val back to Derek and the others return to their visitors, too. Adam was a single man, and his brother and brother's partner are here for him today. Jasmine's parents and auntie have come to see her, although they are Sikh and don't celebrate Christmas as such, but they didn't want her to be alone today when they knew the other residents would have people coming to see them.

"Look at this, Dad," says Kitty.

"Very nice," Graham says distractedly, and I want to shake him, but I know he's just dazed and befuddled and he can't think straight at the moment. He's not sleeping well, and he's bereft. All at sea, as they say.

"It must be something... otherworldly," Kitty says.

"Don't be stupid," Annie says bluntly. "It's just a trick of the light or something."

"Well I think Kitty's right," says Alex. Surprising everyone, including himself, by speaking out against his wife.

Kitty shoots him a smile. She looks at him a little bit differently. *Oh no*, I think. *Not that.*

"I'm going for a walk," says Annie, and she stands and walks off, without asking if anyone would like to join her. Alex sits heavily down next to Kitty and alarm bells ring in my mind. With no idea of what else to do, I want to squeeze between them, keep them apart, but there is nothing I can do but watch. Meanwhile, my oldest daughter stalks off along the causeway, feet pressing firmly into the soft ground. She seems not to notice the butterfly that flutters up from the grass as she passes by – even though it's a rare sight at this time of year. It flits around her, as though unsure what to do, and then turns prettily, flying over the heads of the rest of my family, and into the safety of the barrow. Annie walks on, angry tears flowing freely down her face, liberated by the knowledge that nobody can see them.

Annie, I try. *Annie.* I used to sing it to her, when she was little, when she needed to calm down. Holding her tensed-up, angry little body in gentle arms, I would eventually be rewarded by a softening of her limbs, and perhaps a little gulping sob, then a head on my shoulder. Release. She pauses for a very brief moment now and then shakes her head, as though she's going mad but no, I think; *Annie, you heard me.*

Graham

W**here** to begin with my husband? This lovely, broken man, surrounded, thank god, by his family. Because without them there, supporting him, I don't know where he'd be. Probably here with me. I'd rather that his life comes to its own natural conclusion.

Life is hell, he thinks. I can hear that thought, clear as a Christmas bell. *Life is hell without her.* Funny, really, when I look back at our younger years, and I know there were times that we would have thought life was hell with each other. But that's marriage, sometimes, as I cautioned Annie, and learning to share a life. And having to compromise, on occasion. It's a lot of working out what's bigger, more important, and letting the smaller things go. I can't say we had the perfect marriage; far from it, and I wasn't the perfect wife. Graham wasn't the perfect husband. But I don't know that any of those things are really achievable, for anyone.

You don't know what you've got till it's gone. Those words regularly ring around Graham's head. Joni

Mitchell tormenting him. But, my love, nobody does. We never – or very rarely – truly appreciate what we have. It becomes all too easy to take things, and particularly people, for granted. But that's OK. You can't spend every waking moment as if it might be your last one, or contemplating just how fortunate you are. Life is to be lived.

The human condition; we are ultimately selfish. We have to be. And you cannot truly see things from another person's perspective, no matter how sensitive or empathic you might be.

Now, though, I have been granted that gift, and it's interesting. I try not to abuse it. I still have a huge respect for people's privacy. But Graham's thoughts and feelings reach out to me; his inner monologue is actually meant for me. He talks to me all the time – sometimes out loud, but usually in his head. He asks for my opinions on things he's doing, and he tells me if I'd like something or not.

He is scared of talking about me too much to other people; worried they will lose patience with him. If he just stopped to consider what it's been like when friends of ours, or our parents, have lost their life partners, he'd realise that's just not true, and that people who really care have all the time in the world to listen. They want to. And sometimes they want to talk about us as well.

Actually, Annie is partly to blame for Graham feeling the way he does. One day, about three months after I'd died, he said to her, "Your mum would have loved this." They were out walking in the autumn sunshine; it was one of those rare October days when the sun sat splendid in the sky, its warmth and light bouncing off the golden leaves which still clung to the trees.

"I know, Dad! Of course she would!" Annie exclaimed. She just couldn't cope with it in that moment. She'd been having her own thoughts of me, and she was feeling ill at ease. Close to breaking point, in fact. But Graham had not seen this, and instead he took her words to heart; he pulled himself back from the world a little then, like a snail retreating into its shell. He thought maybe he did talk about me too much. Maybe it was boring. As if!

So now he thinks about me instead. Thinks about me, and *to* me. And I hear it all, unless I try really hard to shut it out. Because sometimes it's too much even for me.

"We can't take it all on," Kiran told me kindly, when I mentioned this to her. "Yes, we are... here... and yes, we know what they are going through, but we still have to think of ourselves. We still have places to go, and progress to make.

And just like before, we have to distance ourselves a little. No matter how much we love them."

She is like me, Kiran. A similar age, and also a mum of three, although all hers are daughters. I can see she was very beautiful in life, and she certainly is now. She died two years – almost to the day – before I did, and she's a source of great comfort and insight. She is softer than Teresa, or at least softer than Teresa pretends to be. I am lucky to have them both.

But it's so very hard to see Graham, bowed and broken, and not be able to help him. I want to listen. I feel it's my duty.

"You did the duty stuff before," Teresa tells me sternly. "Your whole life. Now it's not about that. You'll see. There are other places to go; other strengths to develop. Graham has your family around him. They're strong together. You've been strong for them. Now is about you."

But I watch him, forlorn and lost, willingly shepherded along by the kids. Just pleased not to have to make any decisions.

"Dad, do you want to come back here for carols later?" Kitty asks.

"Carols?" he asks, surprised. "Here?"

"Yes," Tom says, slightly impatiently in my opinion. "Carols. Here."

"Are they doing something, then?" Graham is the type of person who likes things to be organised and have an air of officialdom about them.

"*They're* not," Kitty says cheerfully, "but *we* are. Val and Derek over there, and a few of the others. We were talking about it over mulled wine."

"Which was a lovely thing to do by the way, Kitty. Your—" He is about to say 'mum would have loved that' but he remembers Annie, and he stops himself.

"I know, Dad," Kitty says, though. Understanding.

"Erm, alright then, yes, that would be nice," Graham says. He feels a tiny fluttering of the festive spirit somewhere deep inside. He's always loved carols, ever since he was a boy.

Then – "You're not coming back for the carols later, Dad?" Annie exclaims.

"Well, yes, I thought—"

"Dad!" she says, tears squeezing from her eyes. "I don't want to." She is embarrassed by this display of childishness, but she can't help it. For once, her emotions have got the better of her. "I just want to be at home." There, now she's said it. Everything feels like an effort to Annie at the moment, and particularly where other people are involved. People outside the family. I understand, in fact, because it's how I felt after my mum died. With grief, you are often given a finite amount of time and understanding and sympathy from people, and then life rolls on again and you are expected to roll with it. Sometimes – often – it is hard to summon up the energy.

But just like that, Graham's little spark of Christmas spirit, which could have taken hold with a little gentle coaxing, is extinguished. "Of course, Annie. I know. I do, too."

Kitty and Tom look at each other, frustrated and defeated.

"Well I'm coming," says Alex. The second betrayal of the day. Annie will not be happy.

"Shall we stay a little longer now, though?" Graham asks, trying to find a happy medium.

"Of course, Dad, we'll stay as long as you like," Tom says, softly, annoyed at himself for his irritability just now.

"What about dinner?" Graham asks.

"Dinner can wait! We'll sort it all when we're back."

Without me there, Christmas dinner has taken a back seat. It's all ready-made, from M&S. Shove-it-in-the-oven kind of thing. I fully approve. It used to be all-important to me, Christmas dinner;

particularly when we were first married. I wanted Graham to know that I could do things as well as his mum had. I spent hours poring over books and recipes, and planning it all out. I was so keen to impress him, it makes me laugh now, and I hope that my own children don't feel that way with their partners. Well, clearly Annie doesn't with Alex – if anything with those two, it's the other way around, although as Tom thought, after Alex said he'd be coming to the carols, it seems that Annie's husband may be 'growing a pair'.

Kitty was all too eager with Olly. I could see it on her face when they were together. I could hear it in her voice when she sung his praises. She was so impressed by him; slightly older than her, and clearly very good at his job (now the youngest headmaster in the county). Already he's looking ahead, aiming for the management positions in the academy his school is a part of. He's also an accomplished musician and songwriter. But bloody hell, doesn't he know it?

Graham and I used to laugh about him, late at night when we'd gone to bed and they'd been round to visit. My husband always was a good mimic.

"Of course, I could have played Glastonberry," he'd say in a more-than-passable imitation of Olly, "but I decided that the school just couldn't cope without me. What would the children do?"

I'd giggle, quietly, if anyone else was at home, and Mavis – in her bed next to ours – would grumble at me.

"Sorry, Mavis," I'd say, and rub her soft fur. But while I could see the ridiculous side of Olly, I did worry about Kitty. She was in awe of him, and I could see myself at her age, when I was first with Graham. Almost grateful, to have found somebody who loved me. I was a late starter from that point of view, and it felt for many years as though I might never have a boyfriend. There were a couple before Graham, but nothing serious, and I had it in mind that what I wanted from life, more than anything, was a husband, and a family. I had a good job as a nurse, and I loved it, but I was ready to give it up any time, for the right man.

As it was, Graham in no way expected me to give up my job. He loved that I was a nurse, and he and his friends used to joke about me in my nurse's uniform, never minding that I was in earshot, and I could hear them belittling the very serious work that I had. I let it wash over me. That was what men were like. Graham, meanwhile, worked in engineering. I didn't even know what he did – not really, although he told me plenty about it, plenty of times, bless him. I just couldn't get my brain to behave and take it in. He wore a suit to work, and got the train in to the office every day, alongside many other suited men, all sitting reading their papers and looking very serious and important. The problem (although I didn't recognise it as a problem at the time) was that Graham may have loved me being a nurse, but he also very much expected me to look after him as well. It's not as though he was unusual in this respect; it's the way things were. Many of my friends got married, settled down, had kids, dropped their jobs for a while.

And then we got married, and still I worked, and we had Annie, and I went back to work – then Kitty came along, and I went back to work. "I don't know how you do it," other mums would say, apparently admiringly, but secretly thanking their lucky stars that they didn't have to do two jobs like I did.

And then we had Tom, and I became ill, and work stopped for a while, and Graham picked up the slack, and he saw just what it all meant, to have a job, and look after a home, and a partner, and now three kids too. He was penitent and apologetic, and he'd cry by my side when he thought I was asleep. "I'm sorry," he'd sob quietly. "I'm so sorry." I thought it was him coming to realise how much he'd taken me for granted, and it was, in a way – but it was also something more.

It's a long time ago, though, now. A lifetime. Tom is nearly thirty, Kitty is thirty-two, and Annie approaching thirty-four. I had three kids under five. *I don't know how you did it*, I think to myself now, and remember the gushing tones of those other mums, and I smile.

Then I press a tender kiss on my husband's cool cheek and I know he feels it, subconsciously at least. His hand absentmindedly touches the exact spot, but he's too preoccupied to really contemplate what has made him do so.

It's fine, I say to him. *It's all fine*. It's water under the bridge.

Graham, always more in tune with Annie than the others, notices her tensing up again as more people arrive. "Do you want to go, love?" he asks, and again Tom and Kitty exchange a look. They know it. We all do. Except Annie. She's Graham's favourite. Not that he loves the others any less, but he understands her best. Admires her most.

But both Kitty and Tom are too kind to mind, really. "Come on," Kitty says. "Let's go and get something to eat."

"And we haven't opened our presents yet!" says Tom, although he feels an emptiness when he contemplates them all sitting around in our front room, exchanging gifts. He really can't be bothered. There is nothing he wants this year, other than to have me back. But that cannot be.

"Yes!" Graham says, looking around at his family and gathering himself a little. Trying to find that little spark within himself again. He is the dad. It's his job to keep his children going. "Let's go home."

"I'll put Mum back," says Tom, and they let him, because he's the youngest. I do wish he'd stop calling that urn of ashes 'Mum', though.

Each in turn comes to say goodbye to 'me'. I stay next to them, looking at them more closely than they would ever have allowed me to in real life. Only when they were asleep could I examine their beautiful faces in detail, and wonder at these people who had made their way into my life.

"Merry Christmas, Mum," Kitty says, placing her hand on the side of the urn and feeling slightly stupid. She returns to the small family group and Alex puts his hand briefly on her arm. If I had hairs on the back of my neck, they'd be standing up now.

"I love you, Mum," Annie says quietly, her long

lashes closing over her eyes and her voice cracking.

"Ruth," Graham says, looking at the urn, and the candle in front of it, and trying so hard to make it make sense. His head feels light, and he looks down to find the ground coming up to meet him.

"Dad!" Tom says, and he and his sisters are on the case, catching their dad before he's had a chance to make contact with the stone ledge in front of my niche.

"What...?" Graham says, and he looks so old in that moment.

"It's OK, Dad," says Annie, taking charge. "It's all OK."

Our wonderful three children support him outside and Alex goes to follow but then remembers he has not said goodbye to me.

"Happy Christmas, Ruth," he says, staring contemplatively at the urn, and he closes the beautiful door that my family designed together. He examines it briefly, looking at the figures. The mum, the dad, the three children and the dog. In front of a house. It's like a child's drawing of a happy family, but made beautifully from stained glass and wrought iron, and I love it. The sun is high in the sky above the house but it's heart-shaped and sends rays of love down on the family and home below.

Alex looks at each figure in turn and his gaze

rests just slightly longer on the middle child.

Oh no you don't, I think, and I concentrate hard on the candle just in front of the door. I need to send him a warning, and I can't think how else to do it. The flame wavers, and Alex looks at it. In my anger at my son-in-law, I've actually made it go out.

"Did you see that...?" Alex asks, but there is nobody there to hear him. Nobody that he can see anyway.

"Good work," says Teresa, clapping her hands.

"Yes, nicely done!" says David.

Their visitors have left them so they've been wandering around, nosying at everyone else's family and friends. I feel pleased to have impressed them, but has my action had the desired effect?

Apparently not. Alex turns to exit the long barrow, and join his wife. Kitty, Tom and Mavis have already begun their journey across the quiet fields. Alex takes Annie's hand, and puts his spare arm around Graham's shoulder. He won't say anything about what just happened with the candle, he thinks, because it wouldn't be fair on them. Still, he feels aglow with the belief that he has just witnessed something magical. Confirmation that, as he always suspected, he has a special place in his mother-in-law's heart.

Nick

As Graham and Annie and Alex walk back along the farm track to the car park, they pass a man walking the other way.

"Merry Christmas!" Alex greets him; too enthusiastically, in Annie's opinion.

"Merry Christmas," the man responds with a polite smile.

"Poor chap," says Graham, "coming here alone. I'm so glad I've got my kids."

"And me," Alex reminds him.

"Yes, of course, Alex. You too. Thanks for being here." Graham, ever the gentleman, feels duty-bound to say this.

They continue on their way while the lone man walks slowly and carefully around the bend towards the barrow. He smiles and greets another family group who are just leaving; they've been to see Charlotte, a lovely young woman who insists that she's not young – "I'm forty-five!" she'll say.

I just smile. "That is young, believe me."

She would be fifty by now, had she lived, and

her sons are tall, handsome but shy teenagers. Both of them walk behind their dad, who has remarried this last year. Charlotte is glad for him.

The man walks past them, smiling sympathetically at the two lads, but they barely even notice him. Tall and thin, with closely shorn grey hair, a brown coat, and sensible walking trousers, he is not much to look at. Not to them, at least.

He stands back as he approaches the entrance to the barrow. Surveys the scene. The muted, flat landscape; fields lying dormant, crops keeping their heads down until they are sure of safe, warm weather, which will be some time off yet. The land is broken by hedges and occasional trees and somewhere back there is the sound of occasional traffic, but it is quieter than ever here today. The man looks up and revels in the reams of clear blue sky. The robin on the back of one of the benches. A buzzard soaring high – calling. He looks further up, sees the buzzard's mate. He smiles, and he moves towards the bench where the robin is. Raises his eyebrows as if to ask, *Mind if I sit here?* The robin escapes to the canopy of the tree, and the man sits down. He can hear voices inside the barrow, and he doesn't want to intrude. Besides, he is in no rush. It's Christmas

Day. He has nobody waiting for him at home. He has all the time in the world.

"Hello Ruthie," he says quietly, in his soft Scottish accent, when he does finally enter the chamber. The last of the other visitors left shortly after he arrived; he had timed his visit precisely to coincide with lunch. He's not one for a big Christmas dinner, anyway. He remembers family Christmases when he was as child; his father drunk and unpleasant. His mother tipsy and tearful. His siblings sullen; he is sure he must have been, too. It was not the Christmas they had read about in books, or seen in films or on TV. There was no *It's a Wonderful Life* spirit in their household. There would have been stockings, at least, dumped unceremoniously on bedroom floors by a dad who made no effort to hide the fact he'd necked Santa's whisky. The children were under strict orders that they must under no circumstances get up before six o'clock and even then they were to open their stockings in their own bedrooms – girls in one, boys in the other. Their mother would be up and preparing Christmas breakfast, and then it would be off to church, where it seemed everyone else was taken in by their dad's respectable appearance; fooled by his striking looks, his Sunday-best clothes and his neat hair, parted and combed close to his head. He would lead the singing, loud and strong, and greet their fellow parishioners afterwards, charming all the women, young and old. Nick's mum would stand aside with the children; she often felt as though she was one of them, the way her husband treated her. None of them dared put a foot out of line or, god forbid, interrupt the patriarch when he was in full flow. Only when he summoned them would they be allowed to traipse back home, where he would waste no time in opening a bottle of wine and without fail accuse one of them of looking at him in judgement. "It's Christmas," he would say. "A day off. I'm allowed to relax with a glass of wine, aren't I?"

When the children were very little, it would be their mum who took the brunt of their father's bad moods but as they grew older he might turn on one of them, instead; particularly the boys. They were gaining on him, in stature and intelligence, and they were growing in confidence, too. Experience had taught them that theirs was not a normal household. Their friends' dads were not sanctimonious drunks. Their friends' parents often seemed to actually like each other.

So no, Nick is not big on Christmas. He told me that when he was first married, he tried, for his wife, who was another one of those fortunate people to have come from a happy, loving home. And when their two children were little, he did his best to make it magical for them, too. He thinks it worked, but he never felt it like he supposed he should. He was going through the motions. This was the approach he was taking to his marriage as well, and as time wore on, his wife began to see the cracks, and realise that his heart wasn't in it. Sometimes, she wondered if he even had a heart. Not that he was cruel, but he just didn't seem very… emotional. When her childhood sweetheart returned from the States, her head was firmly turned, and it wasn't long before she was in the throes of a passionate affair, and she realised what she'd been missing.

Nick couldn't blame her. He was well aware that he wasn't all that she had dreamed of – he was steady and staid, but didn't make her 'feel like a woman', as she'd been led to believe she should. She told Nick this and while he considered it faintly ridiculous, he wondered if that was just something else he didn't get about life. Sadly for his wife, it turned out her childhood sweetheart was also good at making his American girlfriend feel like a woman, to the point that she packed her bags and came to the UK, and Nick's wife was returned to the shelf. She and Nick remained on good terms – great terms, really, once they were relieved of the pressure of trying to make each other happy. They divorced, she went on to remarry (happily, this time) and he stayed more-or-less single.

We met, Nick and I, at work. I went back to nursing when Tom was five, and settled at school. I had returned to as close to full health as I could, and I was missing the busy hospital days. I missed feeling like I had something to offer other than being a wife and mother, and I was angry at Graham. I knew that I needed something positive, which would remind me who I was. Going back to work would give me back my sense of self.

I had no thought of meeting anybody new, and no time for such a thing anyway. My view of relationships had changed incontrovertibly in the ten years I had been married. I had begun with such vigour and romance, and determination. Ours would be a happy marriage. I would not be a doormat, and Graham would not expect me to be. Graham was in agreement; a partnership was what we would have. Except... life. The daily grind. The stresses of work, and of caring for small children, and lack of sleep, and my illness… not to mention his secretary. Because silly old Graham succumbed to the ultimate cliché of the working man. That was what he was in tears about, and apologising for, when I was ill, but it took me a while to work it out. The affair was over as soon as we discovered my illness, and she moved on to a new job, in a new company. But Graham knew he had betrayed me, and risked his home and his family. That is what he is punishing himself for now, all these years later; after all we have been through. Silly, dear man. He has no idea I had a secret of my own. Maybe I should have told him.

But what Nick and I had was not an affair, in the usual sense of the word. We were not Graham and his secretary. It went deeper than that, which perhaps was worse, really. Nick was a doctor at the hospital, and I worked on his ward. A nurse and a doctor – Graham was not the only one capable of clichés. (Tom would be disgusted, or at the very least disappointed, that his parents had not been more original). We worked well together and built up a lot of respect for each other, which grew into something more. We discovered shared interests, a similar view of life, and we made each other laugh. I began to look forward to shifts when he was on duty, and feel disappointed when he wasn't at work. I was happier, and it made home happier. Graham felt better about life, seeing me smiling again, and in his penitent state, he continued doing more at home, as he had become accustomed to when I was ill. We became a better team; something more like the partnership we'd imagined, and I had my secret, just as he believed he had his. The difference was, while Graham still felt guilty, I believed I had no need to feel bad. I justified it to myself that after Graham's affair, I deserved it, and so did Nick. We had both been cheated on, and both been hurt, and besides, what we had wasn't physical; there were no clandestine meetings in hotels, or snatched moments at the work Christmas party (well, maybe one, but it was brief and semi-regrettable). Graham, however, may have felt differently about things if he had known.

And here he is now, my Nick. He is older, of course - aren't we all? - and recently retired; living alone, he has been reluctant to give up his work, his structure, and his feeling of usefulness. It pains me to see his worn, tired face, and the sadness in those kind eyes. I want to put my hand on his; I try, but it's not the same. I don't think he knows I am here. I don't think he sees life (or death) that way.

When he'd pictured retirement, I know I had a place in it. He was never sure what; he did not expect me to leave Graham, and he had his own relationships anyway. I never felt jealous of these women; as I say, my view of relationships had changed. But I do know for sure now that Nick had imagined, and hated himself for doing so, that if Graham had died, I might have found my way further into his life. We might have shared a few years together. It was not to be.

He knows full well who those people were that he passed on his way up here. He knows all about Graham and Annie, Kitty and Tom – even Alex. He's seen pictures of them, knows what they do for a living, where the children studied, what I hope and fear for them all, and my frustrations and my delight, my pride, in all of them. And yet, they know nothing of him.

Well that's not quite true; Graham used to know Nick's name, as I would talk about him a lot in the beginning, when I couldn't quite get him out of my head but I wasn't sure why. He was just so... striking. A kind doctor, to patients and colleagues alike. And so clever; so skilled. 'Saint Nick',

Graham used to call him, with a slightly snide note to his voice, but he knew he did not have a leg to stand on when it came to having feelings for somebody else.

As Nick and I got to know each other better, and spend more time together – on our breaks, for example, or occasionally for a 'decompression' drink at the end of a difficult shift - I tailed off my talk of him at home. While nothing was going on, or at least that was the line I told myself, I felt it necessary to hide him away. I didn't even tell my closest friends about him. At a time in my life when it felt like nearly everything I did was for somebody else, he was something that was just for me.

I sit with him now, this quiet, thoughtful, gentle man, who bears the scars of an unhappy childhood and a life spent just this side of loneliness. He allows tears to come and go, as he contemplates the years ahead. He looks at my niche, the happy family image on the door, and he is generous enough to be glad that my family see our life that way. He will not touch the door, the niche, the urn, but he does relight the candle. He does this so tentatively and tenderly, it feels like an act of religion, although that is something he has no time for. No god, no religion, no life after death. How surprised he will be, when the time comes, to find that he's still here.

At the sound of voices outside, he emerges, blinking, into the world. He smiles at Val and Derek, who have come back with their Christmas dinner in a wicker hamper.

"Hello," Val smiles warmly. "I know this looks a bit mad, but we've done this the last few years – last year we had to eat in the barrow because it was tipping it down!"

Nick smiles. "Typical festive weather, eh?"

"Yes, not quite snow falling upon snow," Derek smiles as he points to a flat piece of ground near the pond. "That should be OK," he says, and he goes to lay out the blanket, and the plates, and glasses – producing a bottle of champagne. "We've a spare glass," he says to Nick. "Would you like one?"

Nick is about to say no, but – *go on* – I whisper, and it seems to work. "Go on then," he says warmly. "That's very kind of you."

"Not at all," Derek says. He pops open the champagne while Val collects Teresa's urn, and brings it out, placing it lovingly in the centre of the blanket, amongst the foil-wrapped plates of roast potatoes, carrots and parsnips, and nut roast. A trifle, fat with jelly and custard, wobbles temptingly in a plastic bowl.

They brought their dinner here the first Christmas after Teresa had died, finding they just couldn't eat at home. It was Val's idea; somehow rallying around for Derek's sake, although her own heart was cracked all the way through. Now it's just what they do, and they have come to look forward to it.

"Would you like to eat with us?" they ask, but that is a step too far.

"No, no, you enjoy yourselves," Nick says, wondering if that is the right thing to say, but these seem like people determined to enjoy every last drop of life that they can.

"You're welcome to join us, or do whatever you need to do," Val says kindly, sensing Nick's politeness. He is wondering where to put himself. He really wants to be alone, but he also really doesn't want to appear rude. "Sometimes if I'm here alone, I'll sit on one of the benches and just watch the world here."

"I might just do that," he says, grateful for the direction.

"She's very intuitive," Teresa says to me. She is beaming, like a boarding school child whose parents have come for a second visit.

"She is lovely," I say, and I follow Nick –

champagne glass in hand – across to the bench.

His eyes scan the scene before him, the patchwork of farmland and the eventual height of the follies in the distance, which provide a welcome break to the horizon. In the bare branches of the tree, a gang of tiny birds fly back and forth, twittering with excitement. They're like children allowed into the school playground, Nick thinks fondly, his mind going to his own children – grown-up now, with children of their own. He doesn't merit Christmas day with them, but he'll see them tomorrow, and that's fine by him. They believe that he left them just because he didn't want to be with them anymore. They see him as married to his work, and they know nothing of their mum's affair. They never will, if Nick has his way.

The birds make Nick smile, and the bubbles in his glass help him relax. In time, Derek comes and refills it. The generosity of this small act makes me swell with happiness and hope.

Surveying the scene, Nick says, "Peace on earth and good will to all men," raising his glass to Teresa's son.

"Exactly," Derek says. "Cheers."

Nick sits, and sips, and watches the world, as Val suggested. When she and Derek go to leave,

Nick still hasn't finished his second drink. "Take your time," Val says, seeing he's about to down the rest of it. "We're coming back later, for carols. Leave the glass. Or come and join us!"

"That's so kind of you," Nick says. "Really."

And then they are gone, and it is just Nick, and the barrow. And me.

He sits, he sees, he sighs. He cries again, a little. And then he shivers, realising the sun is almost slipping away and he's cold. He walks back into the barrow.

"Goodbye, Ruth." He says this louder than he'd said his greeting, and the stone walls seem to ring with his voice. "Goodbye," he says again, knowing he never got to say it properly in life. He turns on his heel and leaves, resolute. As he passes the bench where he'd sat, he sees the empty glass, and remembers the kindness of strangers. It puts just the tiniest spring in his step as he walks back through the burgeoning darkness, towards the occasional headlights of passing cars. An owl glides coolly above his head, but he does not notice. His eyes are full of tears, but his heart is full of love.

Christmas Night

I am delighted but not surprised to see Graham and Annie arrive with the others, in time for the carols. There are no surprises anymore. I knew they were on their way.

They'd discussed it over lunch, Graham gently asking his oldest daughter if she might change her mind.

She sulked a little, and mulled it over while she chewed her dinner, ignoring her brother's and sister's pleas to put on her Christmas hat and get into the spirit of things. Why was it so easy for them, she wondered angrily, but she already knew that it wasn't. They were just doing their best. They were doing what I'd asked them to do, in fact – to try and carry on enjoying things, and having fun. To appreciate life.

It is this thought, this memory, that made up Annie's mind for her. "Alright then," she said. "I'll do it. But we won't stay for long, OK?"

"OK," they all agreed, and Alex put his hand on hers, as if to say he was proud of her, but she pulled her hand away. I know he shouldn't be looking at Kitty the way he sometimes does, but she can be a whole lot nicer to him than his wife is. He tried to look like he wasn't bothered, but he was a bit embarrassed. Tom, however, put a kind hand on Alex's shoulder. *We know*, it said. *We understand.* Alex felt a bit better.

He felt better still when, after dinner, Annie put her hands on his shoulders and a kiss on his lips.

"What was that for?" he asked.

"It's Christmas isn't it?" she smiled at him, and he felt the familiar warmth flood through him at being once more in her favour.

Cecily, who has come along with just her dad this time, to blow out the candles and tidy up if necessary – though this is never, ever necessary, as people are unfailingly respectful of this space – is surprised to hear voices, and the twang of a guitar being tuned up. They round the corner to be greeted by the sight of familiar faces lit up by torches and lanterns; cheeks rosy from the cold, and a few Christmas drinks, smiling at her as she approaches. Every one of these people has been the recipient of her calm kindness, either when their loved ones were ill, or after their deaths – more often than not, both.

"Here she is!" Val, a natural leader, says. "Will you stay for carols?"

"Oh, wow! I'd love to… Dad…?" Cecily turns to him, hoping he'll say yes.

Of course, he does. Anything for his beloved daughter. He knows his wife won't mind. She might, he suspects, actually enjoy having the house to herself for a while longer. Ever the thoughtful one, though, he texts her so that she knows what's going on, and won't worry.

Tom, with his guitar, smiles at Cecily, and something clicks. That would be good, I think.

"Let's all choose a carol," Val suggests loudly to the gathered group. "Something maybe that was a favourite of our loved ones."

O Little Town of Bethlehem, I think, willing one of my family to have remembered this about me. Tom plays the first line on his guitar, smiling at his sisters. "Yes, Tom," says his dad, while the girls remember me singing this to them on Christmas Eves, smiling at them sweetly while desperate for them to actually fall asleep so I could go downstairs and get on with the wrapping and placing of presents. Always kicking myself for not having the forethought to have wrapped them before then. *Next year*, I'd promise myself.

An owl – the very same that passed over Nick's head earlier – calls from the oak tree, and does not have to wait long for an answering call not too far away. The people hear, and smile at each other, although Samantha – Terry and June's granddaughter – pulls herself close in towards her parents, feeling the reassuring, soft warmth of her mum's coat. She is not too sure about this place in the dark, but as the music begins, she feels better. She hopes they'll sing Little Donkey because she sang it in her Christmas play, and knows all the words.

They begin with In the Bleak Midwinter, for Teresa, which makes many people cry, and Away in a Manger makes Sally, Samantha's mum, want to pick her daughter up and cradle her; to have her as a baby once more, just for a few precious moments. Then comes a rousing rendition of Hark the Herald Angels Sing. And then it's our turn. My carol. O Little Town of Bethlehem. I always loved the chorus, for some reason. I was cynical, sometimes, about Christmas and how shallow it could be, that there was just one day when people were so focused on peace and good will to all men, and yet these words touched me, and I wanted the magic to be real.

I savour it, aware of each and every one of the people who I love here, as the words come forth on clouds of breath which rise up into the still, silent air, and away across the fields.

The church bells in the next village begin to chime and it feels to everyone like a charmed moment. Cecily remembers the shooting star from this morning. She smiles, and shivers.

They close with Joy to the World, which seems quite fitting, and means that they end on a high.

As the visitors begin to take their leave, wishing each other well, they thank Cecily for everything, and she and her dad go into the barrow, to perform a reversal of this morning's actions. Close the place down for the night. I am pleased to see my family follow them in, to help. Pleased further to see Tom glance at Cecily again. I will watch for progress with interest.

"You guys get on your way," she says kindly.

"Are you sure?" asks Graham, who feels like he should stay, but also is exhausted now, his eyes dry from the tears and the tiredness. Maybe tonight he will sleep, he thinks.

"Of course."

They too wish her and her dad a happy Christmas, and then all is quiet. Cecily's dad watches her, blowing out the candles and leaving those in front of the occupied niches till last. "Goodnight," she says to each of us, "Happy Christmas."

And as the last flame goes out, darkness fills the

spaces that the light had discovered, working its way into the tiny indents and scratches of the creamy stone walls, ceilings and pillars. Cecily inhales, slowly, imagining for a moment that she can hear us; the collective breath of the long barrow. Her dad stands in the doorway and turns on the torch of his phone.

"Come on," he smiles. "Your mum will be waiting for us."

They step outside and she closes the door while he holds the phone so that Cecily can see what she's doing as she locks up. The light sweeps around the inside of the barrow and Cecily peers in, taking a good look round at all the niches, thinking of us all and our families, and wishing us well. Then she slips her arm into her dad's, and the two of them trek back along the path, knowing that we are tucked safely in for the night.

Under the starry sky, a thin layer of frost crackles across the sleepy ground, making the two mounds of the long barrow sparkle in the light of the moon.

Beneath, we are quiet; contemplative, remembering the day. But despite the dark, cold winter's night outside, here in the heart of the chambers there is only warmth.

O Little Town of Bethlehem
How still we see thee lie.
Above thy deep and dreamless sleep,
The silent stars go by.
Yet in thy dark streets shineth
The everlasting light.
The hopes and fears of all the years
Are met in thee tonight.

What Comes Next

First Christmas is a one-off, but it is also the beginning of something new.

What Comes Next is a series that tells the story of Ruth and her family after her death; all narrated by Ruth, with her unique insights into her husband and children, and the people and situations they encounter after she has gone.

Look out for book number one in early 2024.

Acknowledgements

As I write this it is only two days since my final Coming Back to Cornwall book – *Shifting Sands* – was published. Just like that series, *First Christmas* was not really planned, but once the idea began to form in my mind I found it very hard to stop writing. I knew I wanted to publish it before Christmas (which might sound slightly cynical and commercial but also, I wanted it to reach people who might appreciate it. I have experienced three Christmases so far since my mum died and I know how painful this time of year can be when times are not so happy).

I will start by thanking my trusty team of kind, generous beta readers, who had very little warning of this coming their way but who got stuck in and gave up their time, and offered very valuable feedback to me. Thank you to Tracey Shaw, Rebecca Leech, Sandra Francis, Marilynn Wrigley, Jean Crowe, Alison Lassey, Kate Jenkins, Ginnie Ebbrell, Amanda Tudor, Mandy Chowney-Andrews, Sheila Setter and Hilary Kerr. To Roz Osborn, I'm sorry I didn't check that you had got my email!

I also owe thanks as ever to my dad, Ted Rogers, who has again read and offered his valuable feedback. I am lucky to have many great supporters, but I think Dad is probably number one!

To Bev Edmeades, who was kind enough to meet me at the long barrow the first time I visited – and to Susan and Martin who I also met there that day – a huge thank you. You may not remember as clearly as I do sitting in the chamber, talking about anything and everything. Your openness and easiness were very much appreciated, and I don't think I'll ever forget that hour or two I spent there.

To Toby Angel, huge thanks for your support for and interest in this project, and for the beautiful pictures.

And to Tim Ashton at Soulton Hall, who not only has great ideas but actually makes them happen! Thank you, for your support for this project and also for being so open to the local community in so many ways.

Lastly, thank you to my mum, Rosemary Rogers, who actually talked about the long barrow when she was ill, which led me to make that first visit there. It has inspired me in so many ways, just as she always did, and always will.

Coming Back to Cornwall

Books One to Ten

Available in print and on Kindle

The whole Coming Back to Cornwall series is being made into audiobooks so you that you can listen to the adventures of Alice, Julie and Sam while you drive, cook, clean, go to sleep... whatever, wherever!

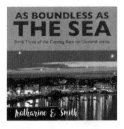

Books One to Five are available now!

Connections

Books One to Three

Available in print and on Kindle

Writing the Town Read -
Katharine's first novel. "I seriously
couldn't put it down and would
recommend it to anyone who doesn't
like chick lit, but wants a great story."

Looking Past - a
story of motherhood, and growing
up without a mother. "Despite the
tough topic the book is full of love,
friendships and humour. Katharine
Smith cleverly balances emotional
storylines with strong characters and
witty dialogue, making this a
surprisingly happy book to read."

Amongst Friends - a back-to-front
tale of friendship and family, set in
Bristol.

"An interesting, well written book,
set in Bristol which is lovingly
described, and with excellent
characterisation. Very enjoyable."

Printed in Great Britain
by Amazon

32367210R00058